Hymns of the Old Camp Ground

by
Wayne Erbsen

Order Number: NGB-960   ISBN 978-1-883206-56-7
Library of Congress Control Number: 2008930903

Come visit us at www.nativeground.com

Contents

Contents

Holiness camp meeting, Shooting Creek Township, Clay County, N.C.

Photo by Gideon T. Laney, Courtesy of David C. Anderson

Hymns of the Old Camp Ground

Welcome Pilgrim! Come gather in close to the fire and warm yourself. We're set to begin the singing, so you showed up at our camp meeting just in the nick of time. Pull up a stump and sit over there by the firelight so you can see your hymn book, if you brought one. No use fumbling through the words. If you didn't bring one, just settle back and join in with the rest of the singers. We'll sing a new kind of camp-meeting song that's so simple you'll never miss your old hymn book. By the time we're done, we'll sing the bark off of every tree in the county. In fact, we're going to sing by the "letter method." So take a deep breath, rear back, and let 'er fly.

Before we commence to sing, let's take a look back to an earlier time on the old frontier. Those who made the journey west of the Allegheny Mountains traveled light, carrying little more than an axe, a shovel, maybe a fiddle, and of course, the family Bible. They also brought memories of religious songs and hymns that they had known since childhood. If only they could join with others in singing these songs once again. For many, their prayers were answered when word spread of an old-time revival to be held in the Kentucky wilderness on the

Courtesy of Jim Bollman

banks of the Gasper River in July of 1800. With much excitement and anticipation, hundreds of people made the journey from as far away as North Carolina and Virginia. Some pilgrims traveled alone on horseback, while others walked or carried their entire family by wagon, often with a milk cow in tow. What followed was several glorious days of camping by the river and meeting friends old and new, hearing impassioned sermons of fire-and-brimstone preachers, and gathering together in song.

Hymns of the Old Camp Ground

The folks who traveled to the early camp meetings came from a variety of churches and religious backgrounds that included Baptists, Methodists and Presbyterians, among others. Song leaders soon found that there was no shared body of religious song that all had in common. Even if there were enough hymn books to go around, singing out of them would be challenging in the dim light of pine knot torches and flickering campfires and the fact that many settlers did not read or write. To overcome these obstacles, song leaders came up with a new kind of hymn that enabled throngs of worshipers to join together in song. Their basic bag of tools included repetition and simplicity. Out of necessity they created singable choruses that repeated simple phrases or lines of verse from older hymns or from the Bible. A few "hallelujahs" might be inserted in a line to add punch. Over time, choruses evolved that were so simple that virtually anyone could join in. These camp meeting songs soon became a powerful force at backwoods revivals.

As camp-meeting revivals flourished on the frontier and more of these types of songs were created, several Methodist publishers seized the opportunity and produced songbooks to appeal to these worshipers. Between 1805 and 1843 at least seventeen camp-meeting songbooks were published. The most popular of these books was *The Pilgrim's Songster*, which sold at least 10,000 copies from 1810 -1828, no small potatoes.

Hymns of the Old Camp Ground is nothing less than a feast of your favorite old-time hymns and gospel songs. For certain, many of these well-worn songs are no stranger to you. You've been singing a number of them for years and probably know every word by heart. Others may be new to you, but even the youngest song in the bunch is old enough to have sprouted whiskers and walk with a limp. As you turn the pages, you'll

FOR THE CAMP MEETING

The Messrs. Gowen, during the next week, to accommodate our citizens who may wish to attend the Camp Meeting at Kennebunk, will run Coaches

Three times a Day

Between Biddeford and the Camp ground; Leaving Biddeford at 7 o'clock in the morning, at 1 and at 7 in the evening Coaches leaving the Camp ground for return immediately after the close of each service.

☞ Names may be left at the Biddeford House, Dr. Rohie's, Berry & Jellison's, Dr. Luke Hill's, and at the house of Samuel Tripp, and passengers will be promptly called for.

Fare,----25 Cents each way.

find hymns of all shapes and colors. Don't be surprised if you bump into traditional hymns, spirituals, humorous religious songs and traditional gospel songs. You'll find that one thing binds this diverse gang of songs together. They've all been touched in some way by the spirit of the camp meetings that were held in Kentucky and North Carolina over two hundred years ago.

A Beautiful Life

William M. Golden   1918   William M. Golden

This favorite old gospel song is written in the call-and-response style, which is similar to the practice called "lining out," where a song leader speaks or sings a phrase and the congregation echoes it back. It was first recorded by Smith's Sacred Singers on April 5, 1927, but the North Georgia Four called it "Each Day I'll Do A Golden Deed" for their July, 1928, recording. "A Beautiful Life" features a bass lead on the first two lines of the chorus. After that, the lead vocal takes over.

A Beautiful Life

Each day I'll do a golden deed
By helping those who are in need.
My life on earth is but a span
And so I'll do the best I can.

Life's evening sun is sinking low
A few more days and I must go.
To meet the deeds that I have done
Where there will be no setting sun.

To be a child of God each day
My light must shine along the way.
I'll sing His praise while ages roll
And strive to help some troubled soul. (Chorus)

The only life that will endure
Is one that's kind and good and pure.
And so for God I'll take my stand
Each day I'll lend a helping hand. (Chorus)

I'll help some one in time of need
And journey on with rapid speed
I'll help the sick, the poor and weak
And words of kindness to them speak. (Chorus)

While going down life's weary road
I'll try to lift some traveler's load.
I'll try to turn the night to day
Make flowers bloom along the way. (Chorus)

Ain't Gonna Lay My Armor Down

Although the name of the composer of "Ain't Gonna Lay My Armor Down" has long been forgotten, the song has such a strong camp-meeting flavor that you can practically smell the campfire smoke. It was first recorded by McVay and Johnson in Johnson City, Tennessee, on October 18, 1928. The Kentucky Coon Hunters recorded it on June 17, 1931. More recently, it's been done in bluegrass style by Jim Mills on his 1998 CD entitled "Bound to Ride."

I'm gonna sing and shout and pray,
I'm gonna sing and shout and pray,
I'm gonna sing and shout and pray 'til He comes,
I'm gonna sing and shout and pray,
I'm gonna sing and shout and pray,
I'm gonna sing and shout and pray 'til He comes. (Chorus)

Ain't gonna run when the battle gets hot,
Ain't gonna run when the battle gets hot,
Ain't gonna run when the battle gets hot, 'til He comes,
Ain't gonna run when the battle gets hot,
Ain't gonna run when the battle gets hot,
Ain't gonna run when the battle gets hot, 'til He comes. (Chorus)

Amazing Grace

John Newton   1779   Anonymous folk tune

It is hard to think of a hymn that can rival "Amazing Grace" for its universal popularity. The lyrics were composed by John Newton (1728-1807), rector of a parish in Olney, England. The first printing of "Amazing Grace" was in 1779 in a hymnal entitled *Olney Hymns* with the title "Faith's Review and Expectation." The lyrics later became attached to the tune "Harmony Grove," as first published in 1829 in *Columbian Harmony.* With the publication of *The Southern Harmony* in 1835, the tune and lyrics were finally put together, but with the title "New Britain."

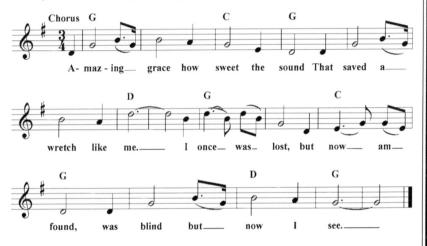

A- maz - ing— grace how sweet the sound That saved a— wretch like me.— I once— was— lost, but now— am— found, was blind but— now I see.—

'Twas grace that taught my heart to fear
And grace my fears relieved.
How precious did that grace appear
The hour I first believed. (Chorus)

Through many dangers, toils and snares
I have already come.
'Twas grace that brought me safe thus far
And grace will lead me home. (Chorus)

When we've been there ten thousand years
Bright shining as the sun.
We've no less days to sing God's praise
Than when we first begun. (Chorus)

An Old Fashioned Meeting

Herbert Buffum   1922   Herbert Buffum

Well, they say it is better, things have changed, don't you know,
And the people in general seem to think it is so,
And they call me old fashioned when I dare to say
That I like it far better in the old fashioned way. (Chorus)

If the Lord never changes as the fashions of men,
If He's always the same, He is old fashioned then,
As an old fashioned sinner saved through old time grace
I am sure He will take me to an old fashioned place. (Chorus)

Angel Band

Jefferson Hascall   1860   William Bradbury

I know I'm nearing the holy ranks
Of friends and kindred dear
For I brush the dews on Jordan's banks
The crossing must be near. (Chorus)

I've almost gained my heavenly home
My spirit loudly sings
Thy holy ones, behold they come!
I hear the noise of wings. (Chorus)

Oh bear my longing heart to Him
Who bled and died for me
Whose blood now cleanses from all sin
And gives me victory. (Chorus)

Are You Washed in the Blood?

Rev. E.A. Hoffman   1878   Rev. E. A. Hoffman

Are you walking daily by the Savior's side?
Are you washed in the blood of the Lamb?
Do you rest each moment in the Crucified?
Are you washed in the blood of the Lamb? (Chorus)

When the Bridegroom cometh will your robes be white?
Are you washed in the blood of the Lamb?
Will your soul be ready for the mansion bright?
And be washed in the blood of the Lamb? (Chorus)

Lay aside the garments that are stained with sin
And be washed in the blood of the Lamb,
There's a fountain flowing for the soul unclean
Oh, be washed in the blood of the Lamb. (Chorus)

Church in the Wildwood

William S. Pitts   1855   William S. Pitts

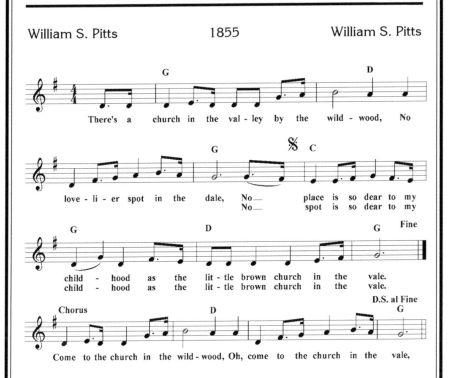

There's a church in the val - ley by the wild - wood, No love - li - er spot in the dale, No— place is so dear to my / No— spot is so dear to my child - hood as the lit - tle brown church in the vale. / child - hood as the lit - tle brown church in the vale.

Chorus: Come to the church in the wild - wood, Oh, come to the church in the vale,

Oh, come to the church in the wildwood
To the trees where the wild flowers bloom,
Where the parting hymn will be chanted
We will weep by the side of the tomb. (Chorus)

How sweet on a clear Sabbath morning
To list to the clear ringing bell,
Its tones so sweetly are calling
Oh, come to the church in the vale. (Chorus)

From the church in the valley of the wildwood
When day fades away into night,
I would fain from this spot of my childhood
Wing my way to the mansions of light. (Chorus)

Crying Holy Unto My Lord

In late November of 1930, the Carter Family journeyed almost due west from their home in Maces Springs, Virginia, to Memphis, Tennessee, a distance of over five hundred miles. On the morning of November 24, 1930, they recorded a song they called "On the Rock Where Moses Stood." The song can be traced to black sources going back at least to the early twentieth century. Bill Monroe recorded it in Atlanta, Georgia, October 7, 1940, but Monroe's version is nearly

The Carter Family

identical to that of Wade Mainer & the Sons of the Mountaineers, who recorded it on February 4, 1939.

Cry-ing hol-y un-to my Lord, Cry-ing hol-y un-to my Lord, Oh, if I_ could I sure-ly_ would stand on that rock, Lord, Lord, where Mos-es stood.

Sinners, run (sinners, run) and hide your face (and hide your face),
Sinners, run (sinners, run) and hide your face (and hide your face),
Go run unto the rocks and hide your face
For I ain't (Lord, Lord) no sinner now. (Chorus)

Lord, I ain't (Lord, I ain't) no stranger now (no stranger now),
Lord, I ain't (Lord, I ain't) no stranger now (no stranger now),
I been introduced to the Father and the Son
And I ain't (Lord, Lord) no stranger now. (Chorus)

Deep Settled Peace

Kate Sturgill Peters   1928   Kate Sturgill Peters

Let not your heart be troubled so,
If to Jesus you will go
And of Him you'll learn to know,
You'll have that deep settled peace in your soul. (Chorus)

Then when death around you lies,
And you must cross the Great Divide,
If you have Jesus on your side,
There'll be a deep settled peace in your soul. (Chorus)

Diamonds in the Rough

C.W. Byron   L.L. Pickett

In the New York studios of Vocalion records on September 9, 1926, Uncle Dave Macon was situating himself in front of a single microphone getting ready to record. When the engineers gave him the signal, he began singing and playing "Diamonds in the Rough," a song that had originated some thirty years before. The lyrics had been written by C.W. Byron and the melody by L.L. Pickett and the song was copyrighted in Pickett's book

Uncle Dave Macon

Tears and Triumphs in 1897. It was the Carter Family's February 15, 1929, recording of the song that helped spread its popularity far and wide. Since then, it's been recorded by the likes of Johnny Cash, John Prine, Merle Travis, the Nitty Gritty Dirt Band and Norman Blake. To my knowledge, no one has recorded all the verses. Here, at last, is the entire song, six verses plus the chorus.

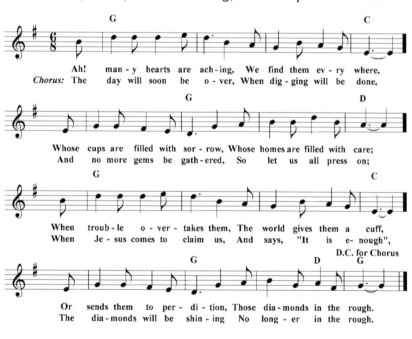

Ah!   man - y   hearts   are   ach - ing,   We   find   them   ev - ry   where,
Chorus: The   day   will   soon   be   o - ver,   When   dig - ging   will   be   done,

Whose   cups   are   filled   with   sor - row,   Whose   homes   are   filled   with   care;
And   no   more   gems   be   gath - ered,   So   let   us   all   press   on;

When   troub - le   o - ver - takes   them,   The   world   gives   them   a   cuff,
When   Je - sus   comes   to   claim   us,   And   says,   "It   is   e - nough",

Or   sends   them   to   per - di - tion,   Those   dia - monds   in   the   rough.
The   dia - monds   will   be   shin - ing   No   long - er   in   the   rough.

Diamonds in the Rough

Ah! many hearts are aching, we find them everywhere,
Whose cups are filled with sorrow, whose homes are filled with care
When troubles overtakes them, the world gives them a cuff
Or sends them to perdition, those diamonds in the rough.

The day will soon be over when digging will be done,
And no more gems be gathered, so let us all press on;
When Jesus comes to claim us, and says, "It is enough,"
The diamonds will be shining no longer in the rough.

One day, my precious comrades, you, too, were lost in sin,
When someone sought your rescue, and Jesus took you in;
So when you're tried and tempted by the scoffers' keen rebuff,
Remember, O remember, they're diamonds in the rough. (Chorus)

O there are many diamonds long buried in the earth,
We pass them by unnoticed, but Jesus knows their worth;
He bids us seek and find them, His message is enough,
He'll save and sanctify them, these diamonds in the rough. (Chorus)

There are complaining people who say we are too bold,
And then there are still others who say we're after gold;
But they are all mistaken, we crave no earthly stuff,
But souls of poor lost sinners, those diamonds in the rough. (Chorus)

While reading through the Bible, some wondrous sights we see,
We read of Peter, James and John, by the sea of Galilee;
And when the Master called them, their work was rude enough,
Yet they were precious diamonds He gathered in the rough. (Chorus)

Now keep your lamps a-burning, the lamps of perfect love,
And unto every sinner point out the way above;
The precious blood of Jesus was shed, and that's enough,
Oh, let us tell them of it, those diamonds in the rough. (Chorus)

Don't You Hear Jerusalem Moan?

While the vast majority of gospel songs are of a serious nature, "Don't You Hear Jerusalem Moan? has been poking fun at religion since it first appeared in *The American Songster* published in Philadelphia by W.A. Leary in 1845. The product of the playful imagination of an unknown minstrel-era songsmith, "Don't You Hear Jerusalem Moan?" was a regular part of the stage show of many blackface minstrels in the 1840s. This crowd pleaser has lasted for over one hundred and fifty years and is still going strong. Among the first musicians trying to capitalize on this novelty song was Gid Tanner & His Skillet Lickers, whose April 17, 1926, recording is faithfully transcribed here.

Well, the Meth-od-ist preach-er, you can tell him where he go; Don't you hear Je-ru-sa-lem moan? Don't__ nev-er let a chick-en get big e-nough to crow; Don't you hear Je-ru-sa-lem moan?

Chorus
Don't you hear Je-ru-sa-lem moan? Don't you hear Je-ru-sa-lem moan? Thank God there's a heav-en been a-ring-ing in my soul, And my soul's got free,__ Don't you hear Je-ru-sa-lem__ moan?__

Don't You Hear Jerusalem Moan?

Well, a Methodist preacher, you can tell him where he go,
Don't you hear Jerusalem moan?
Don't never let a chicken get big enough to crow,
Don't you hear Jerusalem moan.

   Don't you hear Jerusalem moan?
   Don't you hear Jerusalem moan? Thank God
   There's a heaven been a-ringing in my soul and my soul's got free,
   Don't you hear Jerusalem moan?

Well, a hard-shell preacher, you can tell him how he do,
Don't you hear Jerusalem moan?
Well, he chews his own 'bacco and he drinks his own brew,
Don't you hear Jerusalem moan? (Chorus)

Well, the Baptist preacher you can tell him by his coat,
Don't you hear Jerusalem moan?
Has a bottle in his pocket that he can't hardly tote,
Don't you hear Jerusalem moan? (Chorus)

Well, the Campbellite preacher, his soul is saved,
Don't you hear Jerusalem moan?
Well, he has to be baptized every other day,
Don't you hear Jerusalem moan? (Chorus)

Well, the Holy Roller preacher sure am a sight,
Don't you hear Jerusalem moan?
We'll he gets 'em all a-rolling and he kicks out the light,
Don't you hear Jerusalem moan? (Chorus)

Well, the Presbyterian preacher, he lives in town,
Don't you hear Jerusalem moan?
Neck's so stiff he can hardly look around,
Don't you hear Jerusalem moan? (Chorus)

Drifting Too Far From the Shore

Charles W. Moody   1923   Charles W. Moody

Among the more gifted gospel songwriters was Charles W. Moody. Not only did he have a way with words, but with melodies, too. Besides "Drifting Too Far From the Shore," he also composed the gospel classic "Kneel at the Cross." Although his heart and soul was in gospel music, he was also the unlikely source for "Song of the Doodle Bug," which he recorded with his band, the Georgia Yellow Hammers.

The list of artists who have recorded "Drifting Too Far From the Shore" reads like a Who's Who of gospel music. Curiously, Charles W. Moody himself never got the chance to record it. First to commit the song to a record were the Carolina Gospel Singers on September 27, 1929, in Richmond, Indiana, for the Gennett label. Other artists who recorded it include the Monroe Brothers, Porter Wagner, Hank Williams, Carl Story, Tennessee Ernie Ford, Bill Monroe, Rose Maddox, Roy Acuff, Red Smiley, the Stanley Brothers, Emmylou Harris, as well as Helen, June and Anita Carter.

Out on the per-il-ous deep, Where dan-gers si-lent-ly creep, And storms so vi'-lent-ly sweep, you are drift-ing too far from the shore. Drift-ing too far from the shore, from the shore. you are drift-ing too far from the shore, peace-ful shore. Come to Je-sus to-day, Let Him show you the way, you are drift-ing too far from the shore.

Drifting Too Far From the Shore

Out on the perilous deep,
Where dangers silently creep,
And storms so violently sweep,
You are drifting too far from the shore.

    Drifting too far from the shore,
    You are drifting too far from the shore (peaceful shore),
    Come to Jesus today, let Him show you the way,
    You are drifting too far from the shore.

Today the tempest rolls high,
And the clouds overshadow the sky,
Sure death is hovering nigh,
You are drifting too far from the shore. (Chorus)

Why meet a terrible fate,
Mercies abundantly wait,
Turn back before it's too late,
You are drifting too far from the shore. (Chorus)

From Jerusalem to Jericho

Rev. W.M. Robinson   1891   Rev. W.M. Robinson

While the recording industry was still in its infancy, the Garner Brothers journeyed to Richmond, Indiana on November 1, 1924, and became the first group to record "From Jerusalem to Jericho." Uncle Dave Macon, "The Dixie Dewdrop," loved this gospel song so much that he recorded it twice. The first time was for Vocalion on April 14, 1925 in New York City. In Charlotte, North Carolina, on August 3, 1937, he recorded it again, with the song appearing on Bluebird and Montgomery Ward, both budget labels. The song itself was composed by Rev. W.M. Robinson in 1891. The first known printing of the song was in *Apostolic Hymns, A Collection of Hymns & Tunes* published in Fulton, Kentucky, in 1898.

From Je - ru - sa - lem to Jer - i - co, a - long that lone - ly road,

A   cer - tain man was sat up - on and robbed of all his load.

They   stripped him, and they beat him, and they   left   him there for dead, Who
ru - sa   lem   to Jer - i - co, we're trav' - ling ev' - ry day, And

was it,   then, that   came a - long and   bathed his ach - ing head?
ma - ny   are the   fall-en ones that   lie   a - long the   way.

Chorus

Tell   me   who,_____   tell   me   who,_____   Tell me,
tell me who,   yes, who,

who   was his   neigh-bor, kind and   true?_____   From   Je
so   kind and   true

From Jerusalem to Jericho

From Jerusalem to Jericho along that lonely road,
A certain man was sat upon and robbed of all his load.
They stripped him, and they beat him, and they left him there for dead,
Who was it, then, that came along and bathed his aching head?

Tell me who, tell me who,
Tell me who was his neighbor kind and true?
From Jerusalem to Jericho we're trav'ling ev'ry day,
And many are the fallen ones that lie along the way.

From Jerusalem to Jericho a certain priest came by,
He heard the poor man calling, but he heeded not his cry,
He drew his robes about him then and quickly walked away;
Who was it, then, that came along and ministered that day? (Chorus)

From Jerusalem to Jericho a Levite came along,
Unheeding yet the cry of him who lay upon the ground,
He raised his hands up to the heavens and quickly walked away;
Who was it, then, that came along and ministered that day? (Chorus)

From Jerusalem to Jericho the wounded man did lay,
Along came that Samaritan, who was despised, they say;
He ministered unto the injured, took him to the inn,
He paid his fare and told the host to take good care of him. (Chorus)

From Jerusalem to Jericho we're traveling every day,
And many are the fallen ones that lie along the way,
They seem despised, rejected, but no matter what they've been,
When everybody casts them out, why, Jesus takes them in. (Chorus)

Give Me the Roses Now

James Rowe   1925   R.H. Cornelius

According to his own tally, James Rowe wrote the lyrics to over 20,000 songs. That certainly takes the cake! His other gospel classics include "If I Could Hear My Mother Pray Again" and "Love Lifted Me." An Englishman by birth, Rowe made his home in New York State but eventually moved to Lawrenceburg, Tennessee, to work with James D. Vaughan. For "Give Me the Roses Now," Rowe collaborated in 1925 with R.H. Cornelius. It was first recorded in Camden, New Jersey, by the Carter Family on June 17, 1933. Artists who have recorded it include Jimmy Martin, Ralph Stanley and Wayne Erbsen.

Won-der-ful things of folks are said, When they have passed a-way.—

Ros-es a-dorn the nar-row bed, O-ver the sleep-ing clay.—

Chorus

Give me the ros-es while I— live, Try-ing to cheer— me on,—

Use-less the flow-ers that you give Af-ter the soul is gone.—

Praises are heard not by the dead,
Roses they cannot see;
Let us not wait till souls have fled,
Generous friends to be. (Chorus)

Faults are forgiven when folks lie
Cold in the narrow bed;
Let us forgive them ere they die,
Now should the words be said. (Chorus)

The Good Old Way

This song was first collected in 1867 in a book entitled *Slave Songs of the United States.* Although the lyrics were apparently from slave sources, the title may have been borrowed from "The Good Old Way," which was written and published in 1835 by the famed composer William Walker. "Singin' Billy" Walker (1809-1875), as he was known, was the compiler of a number of hymn books, including *Southern Harmony.* By the time of his death, Walker had sold more than 750,000 books.

Also known by its first line, "As I Went Down in the Valley to Pray," this song gained fame in the 2000 Coen brothers' film, "Oh Brother, Where Art Thou?" where the lyrics were changed to "As I went down to the river to pray."

As I went down in the val-ley to pray,

Stu-dy-ing a-bout that good old way. And who shall wear the

star - ry crown, Good Lord, show me the way.

Oh bro-thers, let's go down—— come on down, don't you want to go down.——

Oh bro-thers, let's go down—— down in the val-ley to pray.

Oh fathers...
Oh mothers...
Oh sinners...

Grave on a Green Hillside

Aldine S. Kieffer (1840-1904) certainly earned a revered place in the history of Southern gospel music. An active composer, poet, singing-school teacher, and publisher, he has been called by *The Encyclopedia of American Gospel Music* "the single most important figure in the history of Southern gospel music." Kieffer composed "Grave on the Green Hillside" around 1872, and it was first recorded by the Carter Family in Camden, New Jersey, on February 14, 1929. The following lyrics were transcribed from *The Harvester,* a publication of The Ruebush-Kieffer Co. of Dayton, Virginia. When the book was new it sold for 30 cents.

There's a lit-tle grave on the green hill-side that lies to the morn-ing sun,

And our way-worn feet oft-en wan-der there, When the cares of the day are done;

There we oft-en sit till the twi-light falls, And talk of the far-off land,

And we some-times feel in the twi-light there, The soft
In the years to come we will calm-ly sleep, In a

touch of the van - ished hand.
grave on the green hill - side.

Chorus
Grave on the green hill - side, Grave on the green hill - side;

Grave on a Green Hillside

There's a little grave on the green hillside
That lies to the morning sun,
And our wayworn feet often wander there
When the cares of the day are done;
There we often sit till the twilight falls,
And talk of the far-off land,
And we sometimes feel in the twilight there
The soft touch of the vanished hand.

Grave on the green hillside,
Grave on the green hillside;
In the years to come we will calmly sleep
In a grave on the green hillside.

Ah! the land is full of the little graves,
In valley, and plain, and hill;
There's an angel, too, for each little grave,
And these angels some mission fill;
And I know not how, but I sometimes think
They lead us with gentle hand,
For a whisper falls on our willing ear
From the shores of a far-off land. (Chorus)

And these little graves are but wayside marks
That point to the far-off land,
And they speak to the soul of a better day,
Of a day that is near at hand;
Though we first must walk through the darksome vale,
Yet there Christ will be our Guide,
And we'll reach the shore of the far-off land
Through a grave on the green hillside. (Chorus)

Hand in Hand with Jesus

Rev. Johnson Oatman, Jr.   L.D. Huffstutler

When these two veteran gospel songwriters teamed up to produce this standard of Southern gospel music, the results were much greater than the sum of its parts. Rev. Johnson Oatman was a prolific lyricist, having composed songs like "The Hallelujah Side," "Higher Ground," "Count Your Blessings" and "No, Not One!" The composer of the melody, Leonard D. Huffstutler, was born in Liberty, Alabama, on June 17, 1887, but grew up on a farm in Texas. As a boy Huffstutler learned to sing gospel songs from his mother. After attending Texas A & M College, Huffstutler studied music with J.B. Herbert, R.H. Cornelius, Homer Rodeheaver, and A.B. Sebren. He then went on to a lifelong career singing in quartets and teaching in singing schools for the Hartford Music Company and for the Stamps-Baxter Music Company. "Hand in Hand with Jesus" has appeared in at least thirty-nine long-out-of-print songbooks.

Once from my poor sin-sick soul, Christ did ev-'ry bur-den roll,

Now I walk re-deemed and whole, Hand in hand with Je-sus.

Hand in hand we walk each day, Hand in hand a-long the way,

Walk-ing thus, I can-not stray, Hand in hand with Je-sus.

In my night of dark despair,   From the straight and narrow way,
Jesus heard and answered prayer,   Praise the Lord, I cannot stray,
Now I'm walking free as air,   For I'm walking every day,
Hand in hand with Jesus. (Chorus) Hand in hand with Jesus. (Chorus)

Heaven Above

Wayne Erbsen   1975   Wayne Erbsen

After visiting the ruins of an ancient castle that over-
looked the Rhine River in Germany in the mid Seven-
ties, I happened to glance back over my shoulder to
take a final look at the decaying structure. As I did, my eyes looked
past the castle walls and up toward the heavens, and the phrase
"heaven above" came into my mind. The rest of the lyrics came to
me shortly thereafter.

You've been praying, you've been shouting,
And you think that you are saved.
But when the gates of hell are open,
Sinner, don't call out His name. (Chorus)

Hold Fast to the Right

Unknown   1906   James D. Vaughan

As the 19th century came to a close, professional songwriters had a field day catering to the public taste for ballads that were literally dripping in sentimentality. Today, some people laugh at these kinds of songs and refer to them as "tear jerkers," but back then, these sad laments were serious business. The lyrics of "Hold Fast to the Right" sound like they came right out of the sentimental era of the 1890s when so many "mother" songs were popular. It was printed in *Mac and Bob's Book of Songs*, published by M.M. Cole in 1931.

You leave us to seek your employment, my boy,
By the world you have yet to be tried,
But in the temptations and trials you meet,
May your heart to the Savior confide. (Chorus)

I gave you to God in your cradle, my boy,
And I've taught you the best that I knew,
And as long as His mercies permit me to live,
I shall never cease praying for you. (Chorus)

You will find in your satchel a Bible, my boy,
It's the book of all others the best,
It will help you to live and prepare you to die,
And will lead to the gates of the blest. (Chorus)

Hold to God's Unchanging Hand

Jennie Wilson   1905   F.L. Eiland

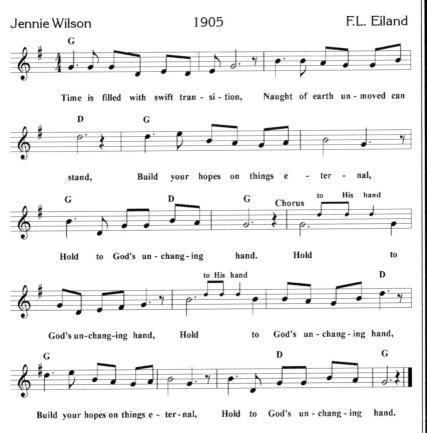

Time is filled with swift tran - si - tion, Naught of earth un - moved can stand, Build your hopes on things e - ter - nal, Hold to God's un - chang - ing hand.

Chorus

Hold to God's un - chang - ing hand, Hold to God's un - chang - ing hand, Build your hopes on things e - ter - nal, Hold to God's un - chang - ing hand.

Trust in Him who will not leave you,
Whatsoever years may bring,
If by earthly friends forsaken,
Still more closely to Him cling. (Chorus)

Covet not this world's vain riches,
That so rapidly decay,
Seek to gain the heavenly treasures,
They will never pass away. (Chorus)

When your journey is completed,
If to God you have been true,
Fair and bright the home in glory,
Your enraptured soul may view. (Chorus)

Home in that Rock

Many of the songs recorded by the famed Carter Family became so associated with them that they are forever known as "Carter Family Songs." Their version of "God Gave Noah the Rainbow Sign," is a prime example. The song is actually much older than the Carters' version and it exhibits some of the repetition that reflects its camp-meeting roots. This version has a minor flavor and was collected in Georgia by Dorothy G. Bolton in *Old Songs Hymnal*, published in 1929.

I got a home in that rock, don't you see, don't you see, I got a

home in that rock, don't you see, don't you see. Ev- er since my Lord set me free,

This old world been a trouble to me; I got a home in that rock don't you see.

I got a home where the gambler can't come,
Don't you see, don't you see,
I got a home where the gambler can't come,
Don't you see, don't you see. (Chorus)

I got a home where liars can't come,
Don't you see, don't you see,
I got a home where liars can't come,
Don't you see, don't you see. (Chorus)

I got a home where drunkards can't come,
Don't you see, don't you see,
I got a home where drunkards can't come,
Don't you see, don't you see, (Chorus)

When I get to heaven I'll shout and tell,
Don't you see, don't you see,
When I get to heaven I'll shout and tell,
Don't you see, don't you see. (Chorus)

I Am a Pilgrim

Even though Merle Travis is often given composer credit to "I Am a Pilgrim," it actually has roots than run much deeper than his 1946 recording for King Records. In fact, Travis apparently learned it from Mose Rager. As folklorist Kip Lornell has pointed out in the notes to "Classic Southern Gospel from Smithsonian Folkways," it was recorded by fourteen African-American groups before it was even a gleam in Merle Travis' eyes. The song was a favorite of Carl Story, who is often called the "Father of Bluegrass Gospel Music." As a boy, Carl Story's father used to take him to the courthouse in Lenoir, North Carolina, to hear his idol, Riley Puckett. It was from Puckett that Story learned "I Am a Pilgrim." Over the years the song has been recorded by such artists as Chet Atkins, the Byrds, Johnny Cash, Charlie Daniels, David Grisman, the Country Gentlemen, Grandpa Jones, the Kentucky Colonels, and Bill Monroe.

I am a pil-grim, And a stran-ger, Trav-lin' through this weari-some land, I got a

home in that yon-der ci-ty good Lord, and it's not, good Lord it's not, Not made by hand.

I'm going down to the river of Jordan,
Just to ease my troubled soul;
If I could touch but the hem of His garment, good Lord,
I do believe it would make me whole. (Chorus)

I've got a mother, a sister and a brother,
Who have gone on before;
And I'm determined to go and meet them, good Lord,
Over on that other shore. (Chorus)

I Am Bound for the Promised Land

Samuel Stennett   1787   Miss M. Durham

Samuel Stennett's famous hymn, "I Am Bound for the Promised Land," was commonly sung at camp meetings in the early 19th century because of its simple structure and repetitious chorus.

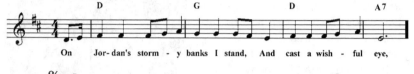

On Jor-dan's storm - y banks I stand, And cast a wish - ful eye,

To Ca - naan's fair and hap-py land, Where my pos - ses - sions lie.
O who will come and go with me? I am bound for the prom-ised land.

Chorus
I am bound for the prom - ised land, I am bound for the prom - ised land;

All o'er those wide extended plains shines one eternal day;
There God the Son forever reigns, and scatters night away. (Chorus)

No chilling winds, nor poisonous breath, can reach that healthful shore;
Sickness and sorrow, pain and death, are felt and feared no more. (Chorus)

When shall I reach that happy place, and be forever blest?
When shall I see my Father's face, and in His bosom rest? (Chorus)

If I Could Hear My Mother Pray Again

James Rowe   1922   J.W. Vaughan

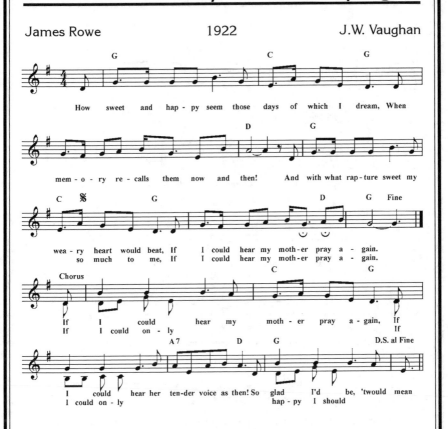

She used to pray that I on Jesus would rely,
And always walk the shining gospel way;
So trusting still His love, I seek that home above,
Where I shall meet my mother some glad day. (Chorus)

Within the old home-place, her patient, smiling face,
Was always spreading comfort, hope and cheer;
And when she used to sing to her eternal King,
It was the songs the angels loved to hear. (Chorus)

Her work on earth is done, the life-crown has been won,
And she is now at rest with Him above;
And some glad morning she, I know will welcome me,
To that eternal home of peace and love. (Chorus)

I'll Be No Stranger There

J.H. Alcon

A.B. Sebren

I'm in the way_ the nar-row way_ To man-sions bright and fair_ With friends I'll be_ so glad and free_ I'll be no stran-ger there_

Chorus

I'll be no stran-ger there, I'll be no stran-ger there, When all the saved come from the grave, I'll be no stran-ger there, I'll be no stran-ger there, I'll be no stran-ger there,_ When all the saved come from the grave, I'll be no stran-ger there.

The Lord will call, both great and small
To mansions bright and fair.
To heaven above where all is love,
I'll be no stranger there. (Chorus)

My path is bright, my burdens light,
I have a home up there.
I'll sing His praise through countless days
I'll be no stranger there. (Chorus)

My Savior stands
   with outstretched hands
He's calling me up there
His voice I hear, I have no fear
I'll be no stranger there. (Chorus)

I'm S-A-V-E-D

I've seen some girls in our town who are n-i-c-e,
They do their hair in the latest style, just b-o-b-e-d, [sic]
They go to parties every night, drink w-i-n-e,
And then they have the nerve to say they're s-a-v-e-d. (Chorus)

I've seen some boys lean back and puff their s-m-o-k-e,
While others chew and spit out all their j-u-i-c-e,
They play their cards and shoot their guns and drink their p-o-p,
And then they'll have the brass to say they're s-a-v-e-d. (Chorus)

I know a man, I think his name's B-r-o-w-n,
He prays for Prohibition and he votes for g-i-n,
He helps to put the poison in his neighbor's c-u-p,
And then he'll have the brass to say he's s-a-v-e-d. (Chorus)

In the Sweet By and By

Sanford Fillmore Bennett   1868   Joseph. P. Webster

Besides composing lyrics, Sanford Bennett also worked as a druggist, superintendent of schools, editor of a weekly newspaper and second lieutenant in the Fortieth Wisconsin Volunteers during the Civil War. Joseph P. Webster, the composer of the lyrics of "In the Sweet By and By," was the composer of the classic Civil War song, "Lorena" and also the music to the popular old-time song, "Wildwood Flower."

There's a land that is fair-er than day, And by faith we can see it a-far; For the Fath-er waits o-ver the way, To pre-pare us a dwel-ling place there.

Chorus
In the sweet by-and-by, We shall
In the sweet by-and-by
meet on that beau-ti-ful shore; In the sweet by-and-
by-and-by; In the sweet
by, We shall meet on that beau-ti-ful shore.
by-and-by,

We shall sing on that beautiful shore,
The melodious songs of the blest,
And our spirits shall sorrow no more,
Not a sigh for the blessing of rest. (Chorus)

To our bountiful Father above,
We will offer our tribute of praise,
For the glorious gift of His love,
And the blessings that hallow our days. (Chorus)

I've Just Seen the Rock of Ages

John B. Presion

John B. Presion

Little is known about the John B. Presion, the composer of the words and music of "I've Just seen the Rock of Ages." What is known is that he was apparently from Kentucky and spent some time in prison. His other compositions include "Running Bear," "Snap a Finger, Jesus," and "Walking Up This Hill on Decoration Day." Both Ralph Stanley and Larry Sparks have made "I've Just Seen the Rock of Ages" their signature song. Thanks to Mark and David Freeman of Rebel Records for their kind permission to print the words and music to this heartfelt song.

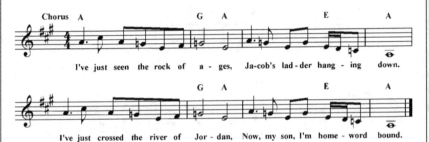

I was standing by the bedside,
Where my feeble mother lay,
When she called me close beside her
And I thought I heard her say. (Chorus)

As we gathered all around her,
The tears begin to fill our eyes.
Then she called me close beside her
Whispered softly her good-bye. (Chorus)

High breeze blowing 'cross the mountain,
Where forever she will lay.
There she'll rest beside the fountain,
There she'll sleep beneath the clay. (Chorus)

Keep on the Sunny Side of Life

Ada Blenkhorn 1899 J. Howard Entwisle

Though the storm in its fury break today,
Crushing hopes that we cherished so dear,
Storm and cloud will in time pass away,
The sun again will shine bright and clear. (Chorus)

Let us greet with a song of hope each day,
Though the moments be cloudy or fair,
Let us trust in our Savior alway,
Who keepeth every one in His care. (Chorus)

The Lone Pilgrim

Attributed to Richard Keen, B.F. White and William Walker ca. 1850

I came to the place where the lone pil-grim lay,

And pen - sive - ly stood by the tomb,

When in a low whis - per I heard some - thing say,

How sweet - ly I sleep here a - lone!

The tempest may howl, and the loud thunder roar,
And gathering storms may arise,
Yet calm is my feeling, at rest is my soul,
The tears are all wiped from my eyes.

The cause of my Master compelled me from home,
I bade my companion farewell;
I blessed my dear children, who now for me mourn,
In far distant regions they dwell.

I wandered an exile and stranger from home,
No kindred or relative nigh;
I met the contagion, and sank to the tomb,
My soul flew to mansions on high.

Oh tell my companion and children most dear,
To weep not for me now I'm gone;
The same hand that led me through scenes most severe,
Has kindly assisted me home.

41

Methodist Pie

Bradley Kincaid was so partial to this song, he recorded it three times, starting in 1927.

I was down to camp— meet-in' The oth-er af-ter-noon to
2. (There's) old— Un-cle Dan-iel, And Bro-ther Eb-e-ne-zer,

hear them shout and sing, For to tell each oth-er how they
with his lame gal, Sue, Aunt Pol-ly and Me-lin-da, And

love one an-oth-er; And to make— hal-le-lu-jah ring. There's
old Mo-ther Ben-der, Well, I nev-er seen a hap-pi-er

crew. Oh, lit-tle chil-dren, I be-lieve,—

Oh, lit-tle chil-dren I be-lieve,— Oh, lit-tle children

I be-lieve, I'm a Meth-od-ist 'til I die, I'm a

Meth-od-ist, a Meth-od-ist, 'Tis my be-lief, Meth-od-ist 'til I die, When

old grim Death comes a knock-in' at the door, I'm a Meth-od-ist 'til I die.

Methodist Pie

I was down to camp meetin' the other afternoon
To hear them shout and sing,
For to tell each other how they love one another;
And to make hallelujah ring.
There's old Uncle Daniel, and Brother Ebenezer,
With his lame gal, Sue
Aunt Polly and Melinda and old Mother Bender,
Well, I never seen a happier crew.

> Oh, little children, I believe, Oh little children, I believe,
> Oh little children, I believe, I'm a Methodist 'til I die.
> I'm a Methodist, a Methodist, 'tis my belief,
> Methodist 'til I die,
> When old grim Death comes a knockin' at the door,
> I'm a Methodist 'tll I die.

Well, they all go there for to have a good time,
And to eat that grub so sly,
Have applesauce butter with sugar in the gourd,
And a great big Methodist pie.
Well, you ought to hear the ringing
When they all get to singing that good old "Bye and Bye,"
See Jimmy McGee in the top of a tree,
Saying "How is this for high?" (Chorus)

Then they catch a hold of hands and march around the ring,
Kept a-singing all the while,
You'd think it was a cyclone coming through the air,
You can hear them shout a half a mile.
Then the bell rings loud and the great big crowd,
Breaks ranks and up they fly,
While I took board on the sugar in the gourd,
And I cleaned up the Methodist pie. (Chorus)

Old-Time Religion

One of the things that makes "Old-Time Religion" so popular is that it is so easy to sing. The verse and the chorus have the same melody, and there is little variation between the verses, so it is easy to remember. It was first recorded by Ernest Thompson in New York City on May 4, 1927. There is little doubt that "Old-Time Religion" came out of the camp-meeting tradition.

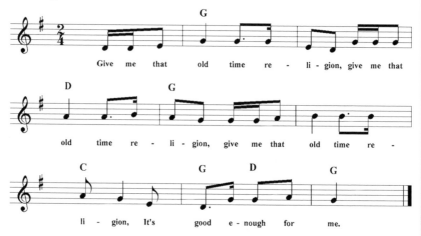

Give me that old time re - li - gion, give me that old time re - li - gion, give me that old time re - li - gion, It's good e - nough for me.

It was good for Paul and Silas,
It was good for Paul and Silas,
It was good for Paul and Silas,
It's good enough for me. (Chorus)

It was good for our mothers,
It was good for our mothers,
It was good for our mothers,
It's good enough for me. (Chorus)

Makes me love everybody,
Makes me love everybody,
Makes me love everybody,
It's good enough for me. (Chorus)

It was precious to our fathers,
It was precious to our fathers,
It was precious to our fathers,
It's good enough for me. (Chorus)

It will take us all to heaven,
It will take us all to heaven,
It will take us all to heaven,
It's good enough for me. (Chorus)

It was good for the Hebrew children,
It was good for the Hebrew children,
It was good for the Hebrew children,
It's good enough for me. (Chorus)

Our Meeting Is Over

Also known as "Glad News" or "We'll Land on the Shore," this song clearly shows the influence of the camp meeting.

Fa-thers, now our meet-ing is o-ver, Sure-ly we must part. And if I nev-er see you a-gain, I'll love you in my heart.

Chorus

Yes, we'll land on the shore, Yes, we'll land on the shore, Lord, we'll land on the shore and be saved for-ev-er more.

Mothers, now our meeting is over,
Surely we must part.
And if I never see you again,
I'll love you in my heart. (Chorus)

Sisters, now our meeting is over,
Surely we must part.
And if I never see you again,
I'll love you in my heart. (Chorus)

Brothers, now our meeting is over,
Surely we must part.
And if I never see you again,
I'll love you in my heart. (Chorus)

Palms of Victory

John B. Matthias   1836   John B. Matthias

I saw a way-worn trav-'ler, In tat-tered gar-ments

clad, And Strug-gling up the moun-tain, It seemed that he was

sad. His back was lad-en heav-y, His strength was al-most

gone, Yet he shout-ed as he jour-neyed "De - liv-er-ance will

Chorus

come" Then palms of vic - to-ry, Crowns of

glo - ry, Palms of vic - to - ry, I shall wear.

The summer sun was shining,
The sweat was on his brow,
His garments worn and dusty,
His steps seemed very slow.
But he kept pressing onward,
For he was wending home,
Still shouting as he journeyed
"Deliverance will come." (Chorus)

The songsters in the arbor,
That stood beside the way,
Attracted his attention,
Inviting his delay.
His watchword being "Onward!'
He stopped his ears and ran,
Still shouting as he journeyed
"Deliverance will come." (Chorus)

Pass Me Not

Fanny J. Crosby   1870   William H. Doane

Blinded by a childhood accident in 1835, Fanny J. Crosby went on to become one of our most beloved composers. She is said to have written over 8,000 poems. In 1868 Dr. William H. Doane asked Crosby to write the lyrics to the theme "Pass me not, O gentle Savior." Together, Crosby and Doane collaborated on over a thousands hymns. "Pass Me Not" was made by popular by Ira D. Sankey at his revivals held by evangelist Dwight L. Moody.

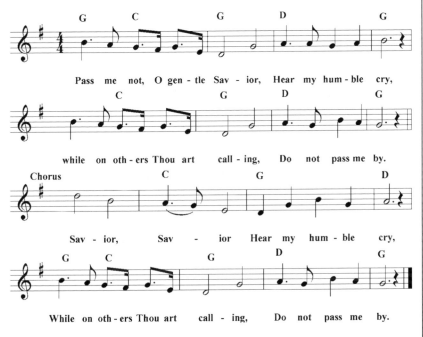

Pass me not, O gen-tle Sav-ior, Hear my hum-ble cry, while on oth-ers Thou art call-ing, Do not pass me by.

Chorus

Sav-ior, Sav-ior Hear my hum-ble cry, While on oth-ers Thou art call-ing, Do not pass me by.

Let me at a throne of mercy
Find a sweet relief,
Kneeling there in deep contrition,
Help my unbelief. (Chorus)

Thou the Spring of all my comfort,
More than life to me,
Whom have I on earth beside Thee?
Whom in heaven but Thee? (Chorus)

Trusting only in Thy merit,
Would I seek Thy face,
Heal my wounded, broken spirit,
Save me by Thy grace. (Chorus)

Paul and Silas

With its simple, repetitive lines, "Paul and Silas" bears the unmistakable stamp of the camp-meeting tradition. Probably originating in the African-American community in the mid 19th century, "Paul and Silas" was first recorded on January 29, 1932, in New York by a vaudeville duet called Snowball & Sunshine on the ARC label. In late 1953 or early 1954 legendary bluegrass singer Red Allen recorded it for the Kentucky label.

Paul and Si - las bound in jail, all night long,

Paul and Si - las bound in jail, all night long,

Paul and Si - las bound in jail, all night long,

Who shall de - liv - er for me? _____

Paul and Silas prayed to God, all night long,
Paul and Silas prayed to God, all night long,
Paul and Silas prayed to God, all night long,
Who shall deliver for me?

That old jailer locked the door, all night long,
That old jailer locked the door, all night long,
That old jailer locked the door, all night long,
Who shall deliver for me?

That old jail it reeled and rocked, all night long,
That old jail it reeled and rocked, all night long,
That old jail it reeled and rocked, all night long,
Who shall deliver for me?

Pilgrim of Sorrow

I am a poor pilgrim of sorrow, Cast out in this wide world to roam. My brothers and sisters won't own me, They say that I'm weak and I'm poor. But Jesus the Father almighty Has bade me to enter the door, Sometimes I'm almost driven Till I know not where to roam, I've heard of a city called heaven, I've started to make it my home.

My mother has reached the bright glory,
My father's still walking in sin.
My brothers and sisters won't own me,
Because I am trying to get in. (Chorus)

When friends and relatives forsake me,
And troubles roll 'round me so high,
I think of the kind words of Jesus,
"Poor pilgrim I am always nigh." (Chorus)

Poor Wayfaring Stranger

I know dark clouds will gather 'round me
I know my way is rough and steep,
Yet beauteous fields lie just before me
Where God's redeemed their vigils keep.

I'll soon be free from every trial
My body sleeps in the churchyard,
I'll drop the cross of self-denial
And enter on my great reward.

I'm going there to see my mother
She said she'd meet me when I come,
I'm only going over Jordan,
I'm only going over home.

I'm going there to see my Savior
To sing His praise forevermore
I'm only going over Jordan,
I'm only going over home.

Precious Memories

J.B.F. Wright   J.B.F. Wright

Completely lacking in formal music training, J.B.F. Wright wrote solely from inspiration. A Tennessean who was born February 21, 1877, Wright once explained, "The words come spontaneously, flowing into place when I feel the divine urge." A short list of artists who have recorded this gospel classic includes Roy Acuff, Chet Atkins, the Blackwood Brothers, Johnny Cash, Jimmy Dean, Duane Eddy, Tennessee Ernie Ford, Aretha Franklin, Merle Haggard, Andy Griffith, Bill Monroe, the Jordanaires, George Jones, and Ray Price.

Pre-cious mem'ries,— un-seen an-gels,— Sent from some-where to my soul,

How they lin-ger,— ev-er near me,— And the sa-cred past un - fold.

Pre-cious mem-'ries,— how they lin-ger,— How they ev-er flood my soul,—

In the still-ness— of the mid-night,— Pre-cious, sa-cred scenes un-fold.

Precious father, loving mother
Fly across the lonely years
And old home scenes of my childhood
In fond memory appears. (Chorus)

In the stillness of the midnight
Echoes from the past I hear
Old-time singing, gladness bringing
From that lovely land somewhere. (Chorus)

Shake Hands With Mother Again

W.A. Berry   W.A. Berry

You just can't beat a song about mother for unvarnished sentimentality. "Shake Hands With Mother Again" was first recorded on December 19, 1930, by the Central Mississippi Quartet. Those who also recorded it include Asher Sizemore and Little Jimmy, Bill Cox, the Carolina Buddies, Wade Mainer & Zeke Morris, Red Allen, and Jimmy Martin.

If I should be liv-ing when Je-sus comes, And know the day and_ the hour,___ I'd like to be stand-ing at moth-er's tomb, When Je-sus comes in His power. ___

When I can hear Je-sus my Sav-ior say, "Shake hands with moth-er a-gain." ___

Chorus
T'will be a won-der-ful hap_-py day, Up there on the gol-den strand,_

I'd like to say, "Mother, this is your boy
You left when you went away
And now my dear mother, it gives me great joy
To see you again today." (Chorus)

There's coming a time when I can go home
To meet my loved ones there
There I can see Jesus upon His throne
In that bright city so fair. (Chorus)

There'll be no sorrow or pain to bear
In that home beyond the sky
A glorious thought when we all get there
We never will say "goodbye." (Chorus)

Shall We Gather at the River?

Robert Lowry · 1864 · Robert Lowry

Robert Lowry's songs have appealed to singers far beyond the church house walls. A few of his compositions include "Where is My Wandering Boy Tonight," "I Need Thee Every Hour," and "Nothing But the Blood." Lowry's inspiration to write "Shall We Gather at the River?" occurred in the hot summer of 1864 while he was a Baptist minister in Brooklyn, New York. When an epidemic claimed countless lives, Lowry assured many of the living that they would meet their loved ones "at the river of life that flowed by the throne of God." He composed this song while seated at the organ late one afternoon.

Shall we gath-er at the riv-er, Where bright an-gel feet have trod;—

With its crys-tal tide for-ev-er, Flow-ing by the throne of— God?

Chorus
Yes, we'll gath-er at the riv-er, The beau-ti-ful, the beau-ti-ful— riv-er,

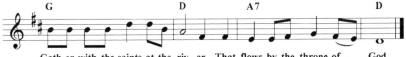

Gath-er with the saints at the riv-er, That flows by the throne of— God.

On the margin of the river,
Washing up its silver spray,
We will walk and worship ever,
All the happy golden day. (Chorus)

Soon we'll reach the shining river,
Soon our pilgrimage will cease,
Soon our happy hearts will quiver,
With the melody of peace. (Chorus)

Ere we reach the shining river,
Lay we every burden down,
Grace our spirits will deliver,
And provide a robe and crown. (Chorus)

Standing in the Need of Prayer

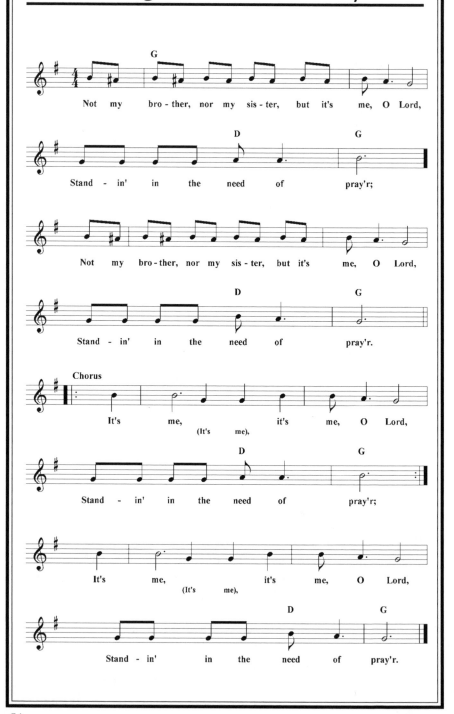

Standing in the Need of Prayer

This well-known religious song appears to have been inspired at a camp-meeting revival. Its simple words and call-and-response style on the chorus make it a natural to sing with an audience unfamiliar with the song. It was first recorded by John & Emery McClung's West Virginia Snake Hunters in New York City on March 7, 1927.

> Not my brother, not my sister, but it's me, O Lord,
> Standing in the need of prayer;
> Not my brother, not my sister, but it's me, O Lord,
> Standing in the need of prayer.
>
> > It's me, (it's me) it's me, O Lord,
> > Standing in the need of prayer;
> > It's me, (it's me) it's me, O Lord,
> > Standing in the need of prayer;
>
> Not the preacher, not the deacon, but it's me, O Lord,
> Standing in the need of prayer;
> Not the preacher, not the deacon, but it's me, O Lord,
> Standing in the need of prayer. (Chorus)
>
> Not my father, not my mother, but it's me, O Lord,
> Standing in the need of prayer;
> Not my father, not my mother, but it's me, O Lord,
> Standing in the need of prayer. (Chorus)
>
> Not the stranger, not my neighbor, but it's me, O Lord,
> Standing in the need of prayer;
> Not the stranger, not my neighbor, but it's me, O Lord.
> Standing in the need of prayer. (Chorus)

Swing Low, Sweet Chariot

I looked o - ver Jor-dan and what did I see,—
Com - ing for to car - ry me home? A band of an - gels
com - ing af - ter me,—— Com-ing for to car - ry me home.

Chorus
Swing—— low, sweet char - ot,——
Com - ing for to car - ry me home, Swing— low, sweet
char - ot,—— com-ing for to car-ry me home.

I'm sometimes up, I'm sometimes down,
Coming for to carry me home,
But still my soul is heavenly bound,
Coming for to carry me home. (Chorus)

If you get there before I do,
Coming for to carry me home,
Tell all my friends I'm comin' there too,
Coming for to carry me home. (Chorus)

Take Up Thy Cross

Rev. A. H. Ackley   1922   Rev. A. H. Ackley

In 1922, "Take Up Thy Cross" appeared in *Rodeheaver's Gospel Songs: for Church, Sunday School and Evangelistic Services*. It's been recorded by the Blue Sky Boys, the Stanley Brothers, the Louvin Brothers, J.D. Sumner, Molly O'Day, the Wilburn Brothers, Traditional Grass, and Little Jimmy Dickens.

I walked one day a-long a coun-try road, And there a stran-ger jour-neyed, too,

Bent low be-neath the bur-den of His load: It was a cross, a cross I knew.

Chorus

"Take up thy cross and fol-low me." I hear the bless-ed Sav-ior call;

How can I make a les-ser sac-ri-fice, when Je-sus gave His all?

I cried, "Lord Jesus," and He spoke my name;
I saw His hands all bruised and torn;
I stooped to kiss away the marks of shame,
The shame for me that He had borne. (Chorus)

"O let me bear Thy cross, dear Lord," I cried
And, lo, a cross for me appeared,
The one forgotten I had cast aside,
The one, so long, that I had feared. (Chorus)

My cross I'll carry till the crown appears,
The way I journey soon will end
Where God Himself shall wipe away all tears,
And friend hold fellowship with friend. (Chorus)

Twilight is Falling

A.S. Kieffer
ca. 1878
B.C. Unseld

Even though this song was originally entitled "Twilight Is Falling," it often goes by the title, "Twilight Is Stealing." Like "Grave on the Green Hillside," the lyrics were composed by Aldine S. Kieffer and the melody by Benjamin C. Unseld. Both men were important pioneers of American gospel music. The first recording of this song, as "Twilight Is Stealing," was by Dykes' Magic City Trio on March 9, 1927.

Twi-light is steal-ing o-ver the sea, Shad-ows are fall-ing dark on the lea;

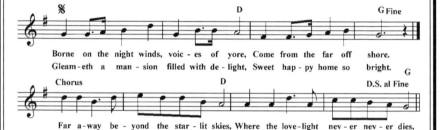

Borne on the night winds, voic-es of yore, Come from the far off shore.
Gleam-eth a man-sion filled with de-light, Sweet hap-py home so bright.

Chorus

Far a-way be-yond the star-lit skies, Where the love-light nev-er nev-er dies,

Voices of loved ones, songs of the past,
Still linger 'round me while life shall last.
Lonely I wander, sadly I roam,
Seeking that far off home. (Chorus)

Come in the twilight, come, come to me,
Bringing some message from over the sea,
Cheering my pathway while here I roam,
Seeking that far off home. (Chorus)

The Unclouded Day

Rev. J. K. Alwood   1890   Rev. J. K. Alwood

A circuit riding preacher who traveled on horseback to churches in Ohio, Rev. J. K. Alwood (1829-1909) wrote "The Unclouded Day" while riding his horse through a long night's journey home. It was first recorded by the Old Southern Sacred Singers in New York City on May 5, 1927.

Oh, they tell me of a home far be - yond the skies, Oh, they

tell me of a home far a - way, Oh, they tell me of a home where no

storm - clouds rise, Oh, they tell me of an un - cloud - ed day.

Oh, the land of cloud - less day, Oh, the land of an un - cloud - ed sky;

Oh, they tell me of a home where my friends have gone,
Oh, they tell me of that land far away,
Where the tree of life in eternal bloom,
Sheds its fragrance through the unclouded day. (Chorus)

Oh, they tell me of a King in His beauty there,
And they tell me that mine eyes shall behold,
Where He sits on the throne that is whiter than snow,
In the city that is made of gold. (Chorus)

Oh, they tell me that He smiles on His children there,
And His smile drives their sorrows away,
And they tell me that no tears ever come again,
In that lovely land of unclouded day. (Chorus)

Walk in Jerusalem Just Like John

Oh, John, Oh John,— now what did you say,—

Walk in— Je-ru-sa-lem just like John, That I'd be there— at the

judge-ment day,— Walk in— Je-ru-sa-lem just like John.

Chorus

I want to be read-y, I want to be read-y,

I want to be read-y, To walk in— Je-ru-sa-lem just like John.

Some come crippled and some come lame,
Walk in Jerusalem just like John,
Some come walking in Jesus' name,
Walk in Jerusalem just like John. (Chorus)

He lifted the cross upon his shoulder,
Walk in Jerusalem just like John,
I'll meet you there the first crossover
Walk in Jerusalem just like John. (Chorus)

If you get there before I do,
Walk in Jerusalem just like John,
Tell all my friends I'm a-coming too,
Walk in Jerusalem just like John. (Chorus)

Warfare

This spooky religious song comes from the singing of E.C. Ball, who used to run a little country store in the mountains of southeast Virginia, near Rugby.

It is available on the recording "E.C. Ball and Ora Through the Years 1937-1975." The song has been recorded by Ginny Hawker as "My Warfare Will Soon Be Over" on her CD "Letters from My Father." Hawker learned the song from Bill & Wilma Milsaps, who live near Robbinsville, North Carolina. The verse and the chorus use the same melody.

My war-fare'll soon be end-ed, My race is near-ly run,

My war-far'll soon be end-ed And I am go-ing home.

My Lord told his disciples,
After I'm risen and gone,
You will meet with troubles and trials,
But by your rebukes I am strong. (Chorus)

You can rebuke me all you want to,
I'm traveling home to God,
I'm well acquainted with the crossing,
And all our ways are gone. (Chorus)

God bless them Holiness people,
The Presbyterians too,
The good old shouting Methodists,
And the praying Baptists too. (Chorus)

And when I get to heaven,
I want you to be there too,
And when I say "Amen"
I want you to say so, too. (Chorus)

We Are Going Down the Valley

Jessie Brown Pounds   1890   J.H. Fillmore

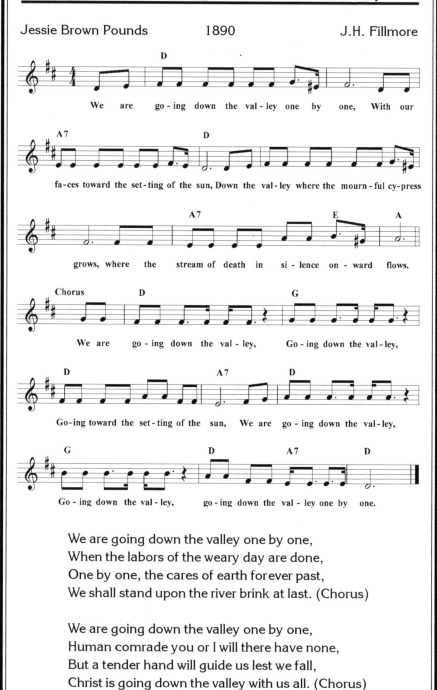

We are going down the valley one by one,
When the labors of the weary day are done,
One by one, the cares of earth forever past,
We shall stand upon the river brink at last. (Chorus)

We are going down the valley one by one,
Human comrade you or I will there have none,
But a tender hand will guide us lest we fall,
Christ is going down the valley with us all. (Chorus)

We Shall Meet Someday

Tillit S. Teddlie

Tillit S. Teddlie

How our hearts ache with grief as we say good-bye, We shall

meet some day, Where no sor-row or tears ev-er

dim the eye, We shall meet some day.

We shall meet where no storm clouds gath-er, We shall

meet some day, By the ri-ver of life, spark-ling

cool and clear, We shall meet some day.

When we've all crossed the stream with its rolling tide,
We shall meet (we shall meet) some day,
In that city of rest on the other side,
We shall meet (we shall meet) someday. (Chorus)

What a glorious thought, as we say good bye,
We shall meet (we shall meet) some day,
In that beautiful home that's prepared on high,
We shall meet (we shall meet) someday. (Chorus)

When I Lay My Burdens Down

Although the exact origin of this old Black spiritual has yet to be discovered, we can speculate that it was influenced by camp-meeting revivals of the mid 19th century. The Carter Family may have "borrowed" this melody for their classic 1935 recording of "Will The Circle Be Unbroken. This version of "When I Laid My Burdens Down" was collected in Georgia by Dorothy G. Bolton for her book, *Old Songs Hymnal*, published in 1929. Artists who have recorded it include Ernest Phipps and His Holiness Quartet on July 26, 1927, the Carter Family on June 7, 1938, and Roy Acuff and His Smoky Mountain Boys on April 11, 1940.

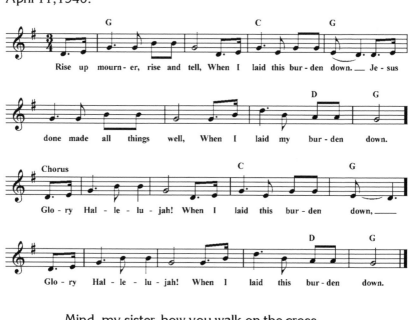

Rise up mourn-er, rise and tell, When I laid this bur-den down. __ Je-sus done made all things well, When I laid my bur-den down.

Chorus
Glo-ry Hal-le-lu-jah! When I laid this bur-den down, ___
Glo-ry Hal-le-lu-jah! When I laid this bur-den down.

Mind, my sister, how you walk on the cross,
When I laid this burden down,
Your foot might slip and your soul be lost,
When I laid my burden down. (Chorus)

My Lord done just what he said,
When I laid my burden down,
He healed the sick and raised the dead,
When I laid my burden down. (Chorus)

Who Will Sing For Me?

J.T. Ely   1922   J.T. Ely

Here are the original lyrics and music to this classic gospel song made popular by the Stanley Brothers and by Flatt and Scruggs.

Oft I sing for my friends when death's cold form I see,
But when I am called will some one sing for me.

Chorus
I won - der who will sing for me When I'm
I won-der who, will sing for me,
called to cross the si - lent sea, Who will sing for me.
who will sing for me, for me.

Where the voice of my King shall call me home above,
Oh, who then will sing the parting song for me. (Chorus)

But I know that at last with our life's record fair,
With trials all past, we all shall sing up there. (Chorus)

So I'll sing till the end and helpful try to be,
Assured that some friend will sing a song for me. (Chorus)

Will the Circle Be Unbroken

Ada R. Habershon   1905   Chas. H. Gabriel

Among the most popular gospel songs in bluegrass and old-time music is "Will the Circle Be Unbroken." The version that virtually everyone sings was made popular by the Carter Family. In New York City on May 6, 1935, they recorded a song they called "Can the Circle Be Unbroken." They apparently took part of the melody and the chorus from the song "Will the Circle Be Unbroken," and added their own verses about the death of their mother. Here, finally, is the original song that was taken from *Alexander's Gospel Songs*, New York, 1908. Among the artists who recorded the original version were the Monroe Brothers and the Morris Brothers.

There are loved ones in the glo-ry Whose dear forms you oft-en miss,

When you close your earth-ly sto-ry Will you join them in their bliss?

Will the cir-cle be un-brok-en By and by, by and by?

In a bet-ter home a-wait-ing In the sky, in the sky?

You remember songs of heaven,   One by one their seats were emptied,
Which you sang with childish voice,   One by one they went away,
Do you love the hymns they taught you, Now the family is parted,
Or are songs of earth your choice?   Will it be complete one day?

You can picture happy gatherings,
'Round the fireside long ago,
And you think of tearful partings,
When they left you here below.

Wondrous Love

Anon. ca. 1811 Anon.

What won-drous love is this, O my soul, O my soul, What won - drous love is this, O my soul, What won - drous love is this, That caused the Lord of bliss, To bear the dread - ful curse for my soul, for my soul, To bear the dread - ful curse for my soul.

When I was sinking down, sinking down, sinking down,
When I was sinking down, sinking down,
When I was sinking down, beneath God's righteous frown,
Christ laid aside His crown for my soul, for my soul,
Christ laid aside His crown for my soul.

To God and to the Lamb I will sing, I will sing,
To God and to the Lamb I will sing,
To God and to the Lamb, who is the great "I Am,"
While millions join the theme I will sing, I will sing,
While millions join the theme, I will sing.

And when from death I'm free, I'll sing on, I'll sing on,
And when from death I'm free, I'll sing on,
And when from death I'm free, I'll sing and joyful be,
And through eternity I'll sing on.

Won't You Come and Sing For Me?

I recently had the pleasure of speaking with Hazel Dickens about her classic hymn, "Won't You Come and Sing For Me?" Here are Hazel's own words about the origins of this song. "I wrote 'Won't You Come and Sing For Me' in the mid 'sixties as a tribute to a people, a place and a time tucked away forever in my early childhood memories. There was a deep sense of humility, a love and kindness that guided these kindred spirits and bonded these common people. Their old style of singing, their old Primitive songs have surely left their imprints on my singing style and much of my writing. One of my fondest memories is being surrounded by the sheer raw vocal power of the whole congregation singing unaccompanied in unison, unleashing all that pent up raw emotion in the notes of a song. It is a sound that could only come from whence it came."

I feel the sha-dow now up-on me and fair an-gels beck-on me. Be-fore I go, dear Chris-tian bro-thers, Won't you come and sing for me?

Chorus: Sing the hymns we sang to-get-her In that plain lit-tle church with the ben-ches all worn. How dear to my heart, how pre-cious the mom-ents we stood shak-ing hands and sing-ing the songs.

My burden is heavy my way has grown weary,
I have traveled a road that is long,
And it would warm this old heart, my brother
If you'd come and sing one song. (Chorus)

In my home beyond that dark river,
Your dear faces no more I'll see,
Until we meet where there's no more sad partings
Won't you come and sing for me? (Chorus)

Working on a Building

This version of "Working on a Building" was collected in Georgia in the late 1920s by Dorothy G. Bolton as "I Work on a Building Too." It was published in her 1929 book *Old Songs Hymnal.* Only the last verse and the chorus resemble the more common lyrics that are sung nowadays. It is interesting to note that the musical phrasing on the chorus seems to have an almost Calypso feel. Although this version was collected in Georgia, it is entirely possible that it originated even further south. After receiving numerous requests for "I'm Working on a Building," Bill Monroe learned it from the Carter Family's version recorded on May 8, 1934. On January 25, 1954, Bill Monroe recorded it as a duet with Jimmy Martin.

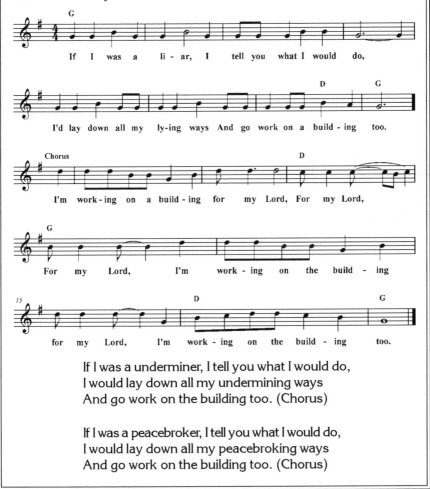

If I was a liar, I tell you what I would do,
I'd lay down all my lying ways And go work on a building too.

Chorus
I'm working on a building for my Lord, For my Lord, For my Lord, I'm working on the building for my Lord, I'm working on the building too.

If I was a underminer, I tell you what I would do,
I would lay down all my undermining ways
And go work on the building too. (Chorus)

If I was a peacebroker, I tell you what I would do,
I would lay down all my peacebroking ways
And go work on the building too. (Chorus)

Index

Index

Press Owensby, Black Mountain, N.C.

Photo by Wayne Erbsen

Native Ground Books & Music

Books of Songs, Lore, & Home Cookin'

Songbooks

Backpocket Bluegrass Songbook
Backpocket Old-Time Songbook
Bluegrass Gospel Songbook
Cowboy Songs, Jokes, Lingo 'n Lore
Front Porch Songs, Jokes & Stories
Old Time Gospel Songbook

Railroad Fever
Singing Rails
Log Cabin Pioneers
The Outhouse Papers
Rousing Songs of Civil War
Rural Roots of Bluegrass

Instruction

Bluegrass Banjo for the Complete Ignoramus!
Bluegrass Mandolin for the Complete Ignoramus!
Clawhammer Banjo for the Complete Ignoramus!
Old-Time Fiddle for the Complete Ignoramus!
Painless Mandolin Melodies
Southern Mountain Banjo
Southern Mountain Mandolin
Southern Mountain Fiddle
Southern Mountain Guitar
Southern Mountain Dulcimer
Starting Bluegrass Banjo From Scratch

Home Cookin'

Children at the Hearth
Log Cabin Cooking
Lost Art of Pie Making
Mama's in the Kitchen
Old-Time Farmhouse Cooking
Secrets of the Great Old-Timey Cooks
Take Two & Butter 'Em While They're Hot!
The 1st American Cookie Lady

Recordings

Front Porch Favorites
Log Cabin Songs
The Home Front
Railroadin' Classics
Railroad Fever
Rural Roots of Bluegrass
Singing Rails
Southern Soldier Boy